Being Patriotic

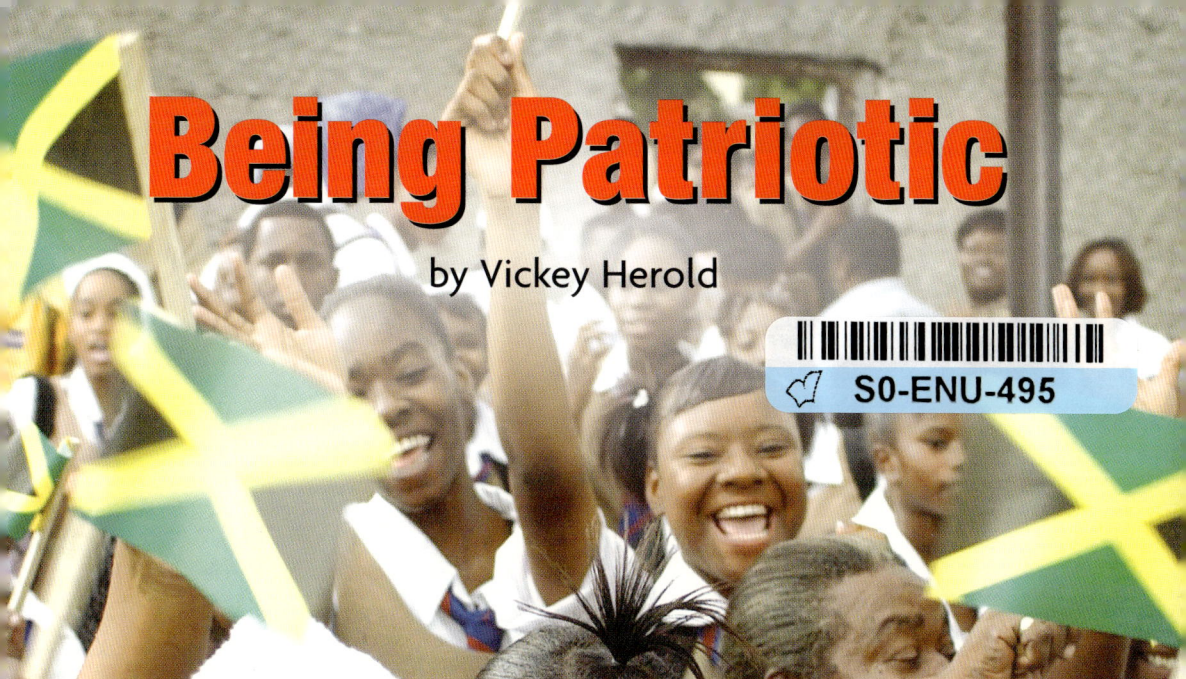

by Vickey Herold

Table of Contents

Who Is Patriotic? 4
What Symbols Make People Feel Patriotic? 8
What Do Patriotic People Do? 12
Glossary and Index 16

I need to know these words.

citizens

country

flags

holiday

patriotic

symbols

Who Is Patriotic?

Many people love their **country**. Many people are proud of their country. These people are **patriotic**.

▲ People who love their country are patriotic.

Patriotic people want what is best for their country. This man was patriotic. He helped Mexico become a new country. This man was the first president of Mexico.

▲ Benito Juárez was a patriotic man.

This man was patriotic, too. This man taught people to treat one another fairly. He helped make his country better.

▲ Martin Luther King, Jr. was a patriotic man.

This woman is also patriotic. She loves her country. This woman led her country for many years.

United Kingdom

▲ Margaret Thatcher is a patriotic woman.

What Symbols Make People Feel Patriotic?

All countries have **symbols**. Some symbols make people feel patriotic. **Flags** are symbols. Flags cause many people to feel patriotic.

▲ A country's flag is a patriotic symbol.

Other symbols also make people feel patriotic. The maple leaf is a symbol. The maple leaf causes some people to feel patriotic.

▲ The maple leaf is a patriotic symbol for Canada.

The Liberty Bell is a symbol. The Liberty Bell causes some people to feel patriotic. The Liberty Bell is a symbol of freedom.

▲ The Liberty Bell is a patriotic symbol for the United States of America.

This tower is a symbol. This tower is very tall. This tower causes many people to feel patriotic.

▲ The Eiffel Tower is a patriotic symbol for France.

What Do Patriotic People Do?

Patriotic people respect their country. Some people stand to honor their country's flag. These people are patriotic. Patriotic people sing their country's national song.

▲ Patriotic people stand to honor their country's flag.

Patriotic people celebrate special **holidays**, too. Many people celebrate the day their country began. Many countries celebrate people who fought for their country.

▲ **Patriotic people celebrate their country on special holidays.**

Patriotic people are good **citizens**. Patriotic people want what is best for their country.

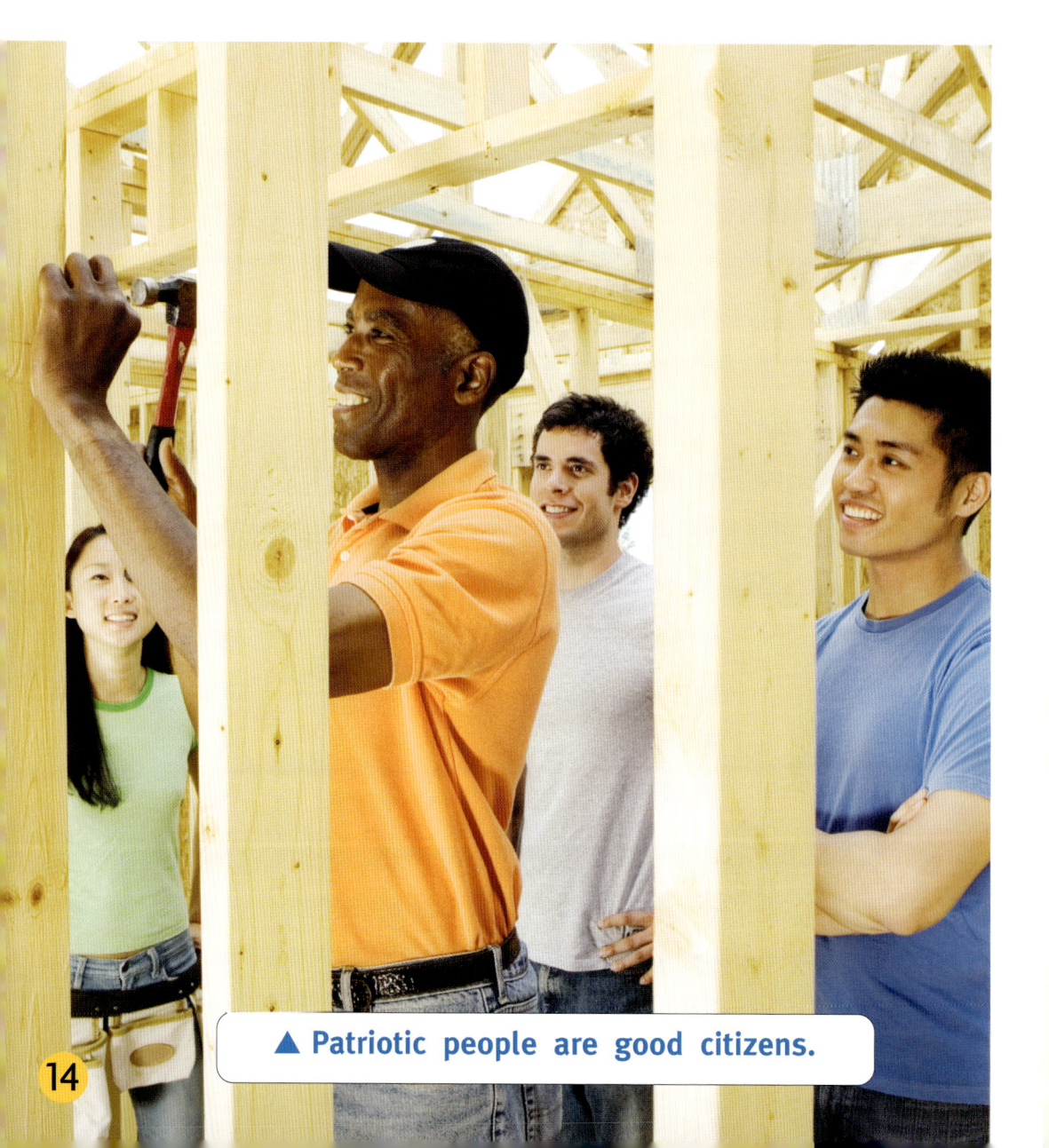

▲ Patriotic people are good citizens.

Patriotic people keep their country clean, too. People can be patriotic in many ways. How can you be patriotic?

▲ Keeping your country clean is being patriotic.

Glossary

citizens (SIH-tuh-zuns): people who live in a country
See page 14.

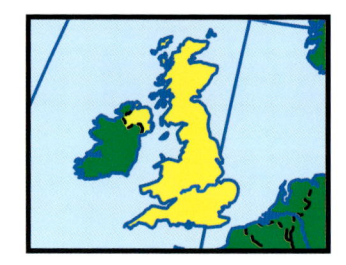

country (KUN-tree): a nation with its own government
See page 4.

flags (FLAGZ): pieces of fabric that are symbols of countries
See page 8.

holiday (HAH-luh-day): a day people celebrate to remember a person or event
See page 13.

patriotic (pay-tree-AH-tik): proud of your country
See page 4.

symbols (SIM-bulz): things that mean something different
See page 8.

Index

citizens, 14
country, 4–8, 12–15
flags, 8, 12
holiday, 13
Liberty Bell, 10
maple leaf, 9
national song, 12
patriotic, 4–15
symbols, 8–11